She Ca[...] Things

Things

Reclaiming Identity

Alexis Preston

Copyright © 2022 *Alexis Preston*

All rights reserved.

Table of Contents

Dedication... i

Acknowledgements... ii

About the Author iii

Introduction... iv

Teacups 1

Born Into This World..3

Changing Points..5

Premeditated Bad Choices...6

Inspired Encounters 8

The Spirit of Suicide..9

Spiritual Attack..12

Rock Bottom-and STUCK...13

A Doctor Without All the Information 15

Broken But Loved...16

More Wrong Choices...17

Working All Things Together...20

Go Home..21

No Smooth Transitions 22

God Brings Me a Gift 23

New Beginnings..26

Tsunami Effect...29

Masking Hurts..30

What's In Your Body? 32

New Developments...34

This Isn't Happening 35

God Confirms 37

Visalia 39

God Brings Me Another Blessing.. 40

Another One on the Way 42

Emergency Changes.. 44

Stuck Between a Rock and a Hard Place 46

Trauma Scars are Stopping Points 47

Medicine 48

Eww, what's wrong with you? 50

Increasing Anxiety 51

Making a Way.. 52

God Uses Dogs 53

Relationships Grow... 54

Training, Training, Training 55

Hit the Fan.. 56

Enemy Attack.. 58

Out of Control 59

Pressing In... 60

The World Shuts Down 61

Truth In Doctrine 63

Breakthrough- The Journey Begins 64

The Wrong Enemy 65

Masked Emotions.. 66

Crying Out 67

God Continues to be Faithful... 69

With God, You Can Do Anything 71

Created for a Purpose.. 72

Now, what? 74

Dedication

I would like to dedicate this labor of love to the one person who has walked with me from the moment our earthly bodies met. Austin, Love of My Forever, thank you for never giving up on me- even when I was ready to give up on myself. Even in the early days, when we hadn't figured out to put God first yet, you helped me discover that there was more to life. You have continued to be a solid rock for our family as my husband, a father to our sons and the leader of our family. Thank you for standing by me and always putting me first. Thank you for always growing with me. I'll love you forever!

-LOYF

Acknowledgements

I would like to especially thank a few key people along my journey.

Mrs. L- Thank you for loving me like Jesus when I felt like no one else did. You helped me get to where I am today.

Lori- Thank you for being my first spiritual Godmother and role model (for all aspects of my life). You inspire me in all that you do!

Arlon and Annette (AKA Austin's Parents)- Thank you for loving me even with all the scars. I believe you had prophetic understanding of what Austin and I would do. Thank you for cheering me on and helping me grow!

Gary- He found me in the deepest of places. I pray that He does for you what He has done for me.

Mom and Dad- My relationships with you have evolved and changed over the years. I thank God that by grace we have all grown from the early days. While we did all make mistakes, I know you did the best you could and I love you for that. I am proud of both of you for your continued growth as people. I love you both immensely!

About the Author

Alexis Preston grew up in Sacramento, California, and she has lived in California her whole life. She spent some time in Southern California getting a college education before relocating back to Sacramento State to graduate with a teaching credential. She has been married for 14 years, and has two sons. She is currently a 6th-grade teacher and leads Youth Ministries at The Fathers House Elk Grove church. Last summer, she earned her M.Ed. in Curriculum and Instruction from American College of Education.

This book is a recount of the Holy Spirit taking her on a journey to discover her true identity and what God says about her. Through the journey, God helped her relive traumas and learn that He was with her the whole time. Through God's leading, she discovered a misdiagnosis that resulted in pressing into God to receive complete healing and restoration.

Alexis prays that as you read the details of her story, you too can find a hope and freedom through the grace and empowerment of God.

Introduction

"We are on a journey," He said.

I must be powerful! Look at all the effort the enemy has put into trying to destroy me, and I have to say, he has a strategy! He worked hard! But now I am not alone and know who I am in Christ! I've learned for myself. No one defines me but God Himself.

This is a recount of my journey of discovery and breakthrough. It is my roadmap of where God was with me all along. There are many instances where it is clear that God was there, but at the moment, I had no idea. This roadmap clarifies how God can use the ugly for something beautiful and His glory.

If it's not good, it's not done. I hope that through reading this recount of my experience, you can also find hope and space to find your healing.

Teacups

I love roller coasters, but the Teacups ride is one of my favorites. The passengers crowd together, working hard to spin the wheel, causing the teacup to spin faster as the collection of teacups spins around each other. I was turning within spinning- my life as the rider rides the teacups, the world wizzes by. As the cup spins, it zooms in and out, getting closer to the other teacups. As you get closer to the other cups, there is a moment's pause before being pulled in another spinning direction.

Quick, zoomed-in glimpses of other passengers in other teacups give the sense of a fast connection before being ripped away. These connections are crisp and vivid. For a moment, what's right in front of you is not blurry. These touch moments are ones of clarity among the chaos, and I have had many of them throughout my life. The speed at which these touch moments occur sometimes brings a drop in the stomach- a feeling of falling with nowhere to fall.

This journey that the Holy Spirit has taken me on can best be described as an extended time of discovery on the teacups ride. Each time He brings me to a moment in time to relive or explain what was going on, I find myself surrendering more freely to the love, compassion, and care of my creator. Though there might be a temporary drop in my stomach as I relive the moment, the clarity that comes from what God reveals is healing and refreshing. I have come to love that stomach drop feeling of falling because I know God is my safety net and harness- I am fully covered.

Even as I write, the Holy Spirit is renewing my life and healing wounds that have accrued and been affecting me for the better of four decades.

Born Into This World

I certainly did not ask to be born into the life that I was, and it took me 36 years to be genuinely thankful for it. We do not get to pick the hand we are dealt, but we do get to determine how we will play.

My earliest memory is of domestic violence; my infant self, propped up on a pillow to witness my mom being thrown into furniture by my alcoholic biological father, my biology donor. Let me take a moment to say. My childhood was not my mom's fault. As an adult, I can see that she did the best she could with what she had.

My mom got us out of that situation and began the task of raising me on her own. At 24 years old and alone, my mom reached out to her mother, a devout Catholic. It was with these two women that I was primarily raised. Within a few short years, my mom met my dad, and they conceived and brought my brother into this world. Let me briefly explain. The man I call dad is not at all blood-related to me. He never married my mom either. He is my brother's biological dad and the only earthly one who ever took an interest in my life.

In May of 1990, my brother entered the world in a whirlwind event that lasted less time than a typical first date! My mom and dad had my brother when I was under six. Once he was born, everything changed. My parents had some good times, but for the most part, their relationship was riddled with infidelity and drama. My brother and I were on a visitation schedule to go to dad's house on Tuesdays, Thursdays, and weekends. I became the constant for my brother as we switched places three times a week.

I look back and can see many enemy attacks in the early years. I can see how our family was under constant spiritual warfare and actively sustained some serious strongholds. As my life marinated in the mire, I began to make choices for myself that helped me dance with the devil. As I was exposed to more and more of the darkness of this world, my brain absorbed what was around me.

Changing Points

My life changed forever when I was in the fifth grade. By this point, I had serious self-esteem issues, no idea who I was, and was overwhelmingly angry. I was confused and felt like I was always running in circles. Chaos seemed to surround me. We were living in Rancho Cordova in a little house with a big backyard. I tried hard to find friends and fit in, but I was bullied at every school. My mom was not the one who encouraged our friends to come over; she would rather us be gone, so that is precisely what I did. I found places to go.

On one occasion in 5th grade, I went to a friend's house for a sleepover. There were other girls there, ones I did not know. I wanted to fit in, so I went along with a foolish plan for the next day's adventures.

Premeditated Bad Choices

I did not want to participate, but in the moment of the occurrence, I got roped in too. Shoving item after item into my bag, the girls loaded me with curling irons, makeup, and cheap jewelry. With each item, I felt tied down to the choice. My backpack was heavy, but the pit in my stomach was heavier. I wanted to throw up and cry simultaneously- maybe my first remembered anxiety attack.

As the security cop pulled out his weapon at a group of eleven-year-old shoplifters, I saw my life flash before my eyes. Sounds intense, I know! But when you are eleven, sudden movement from the belt by someone in uniform is alarming.

"What are you doing?" God's Spirit overwhelmed me. I immediately knew that this voice was different from my internal voice, but it would be decades before I realized it was God.

We were asked to drop our bags and escorted to the store's back room. Our parents were called, and our pictures were taken. After a few short minutes of shaking polaroids, I was famously displayed amongst the other thieves on the back wall of that store. I was officially banned from the store and had to be picked up by my mom; thankfully, nobody called the cops.

That incident was the last straw and prompted a tough decision on my mom's part. Looking into the future to see the devastation that my life could be with a lifestyle of crime and bad choices, she did the only thing she could think of- she sent us to a private Catholic school. It was a sacrifice as it meant my mom had to pay a monthly fee and commit to a certain number of service hours involving yard supervision.

Inspired Encounters

I don't remember everything about Mrs. L, my 6th-grade teacher, but I remember how she changed my life. She was only there with me that first year, but I am convinced God put her there just for me. She broke through to me the way no one else had. She sat me down and shared that God had big plans for me and that I was made for more. The tender look in her eyes provided the peace of understanding that she was telling the truth.

You see, God has shown me that He has been with me all along. He is showing me that there have been several touch points throughout my life that seemingly human people embody the words, actions, and feelings of the Holy Spirit, the guide and comforter. It was one such time. As I think back, those eyes during that talk were those of the eyes of Jesus. The tender love she possessed for me was not that of a student and teacher only, but that of deep love and care for wellbeing.

What Mrs. L did not know was that I was also carrying a spirit of suicide. As an adult, I have studied the Spirit of suicide to try and better understand what is plaguing our youth. The realizations I have been shown about my own life through that process have been monumentally meaningful for me and are a big part of me gaining wisdom about how God feels about me.

The Spirit of Suicide

Kris Vallotton is an evangelist from Bethel Church in Redding, California, who suffered from suicidal thoughts and has done lots of research on the spirit of suicide. It is through the revelations given to him by God that this truth identity journey began a handful of years ago. His blog describes suicidal thoughts as rooted in two possibilities; your soul caused by trauma and a spiritual attack. This distinction might not seem super significant, but knowing where the ideas came from helped me see where God was surrounding me and speaking into my life through the noise of suicidal thoughts. I am no expert on the spirit of suicide, but what I have learned has helped me feel empowered to avoid that spirit.

A spirit of suicide is a form of energy of death meant to take you out. That is the goal. Often the feelings are accompanied by compulsive thoughts. I believe my suicidal thoughts stemmed primarily from spiritual warfare in my early days, but later in life, they came from trauma. In the early days of suicidal thoughts, I would stare at the knife drawer in the kitchen and contemplate what it would feel like to be free of the heaviness that felt like life. As I have gotten closer to the Holy Spirit, He has revealed that early on, the enemy knew I would be powerful, so he has been trying to take me out since birth. Thankfully, through continued empowerment by grace, I have been strong enough to confront these memories.

Now, I have to make a small interjection here. It is not the time to close the book and determine that the author is just cocky or a whack-a-doodle. No! I am telling you that the Holy Spirit showed me WHY

I was being attacked before I could genuinely defend myself. The enemy has been trying to stop me from building the kingdom. He wants me to fail. He wants me to give up and crumble. If he can cause me to take myself out of the race, he can stop worrying about me making a difference. You see, the enemy does not care about age and maturity level. It is the enemy's tactic to try and take us out before we even know he is there.

Mrs. L. had no idea that these thoughts were swimming around in my head, but God did. She had no idea that she was one of the only people with who I felt a connection. Between the pre-teen hormones of puberty and the spiritual attacks I was under, I was a hot mess. The emotional temperature of my life began to rise, and spiritual warfare causing suicidal thoughts was replaced with trauma causing suicidal thoughts. The more passionate I got, the more destructive I became to myself.

Through this recent journey of rediscovering and redefining myself with the help of the Holy Spirit, I have been able to see He has been with me. Hillsong United has a song, Another in the Fire, that speaks to the reliable protection of the Holy Spirit walking with me through my life.

There was another in the fire
Standing next to me
There was another in the waters
Holding back the seas

As I first heard the song, I began to weep with understanding. He has been Another in the fire my entire life. Deep in my soul, I felt the reality that I have a purpose that the enemy has always wanted to squash.

Spiritual Attack

A war waged inside me that caused confusion and a roller coaster of emotions. The thoughts that consumed my mind were the words of bullies and the world telling me I did not fit in and did not belong. I did not realize at the time that the enemy was using what he could to shake me and make me weak. I wanted nothing more than not to feel anymore. Unknown to me, I was under spiritual attack without a way to defend myself. I did not know about spiritual weapons and how to fight the invisible attack. I was unskilled, undertrained, and vulnerable to what the enemy had in store for me. I did not know about the armor of God and certainly had no idea how to pray to put it on. The people around me lacked the forethought and understanding to guide me into spiritual battle, so the Holy Spirit worked on my behalf, like a superhero without my awareness.

My high school years were riddled with self-medication and trying to escape my reality. I learned how to numb the pain, but I never could run from it. While maintaining excellent grades and holding down a job, I silently struggled to survive. I was depressed and overwhelmed. My lifestyle provided me opportunities to continue making poor choices and put myself in bad situations.

Rock Bottom-and STUCK

I hit what I thought was rock bottom when I was chased, captured, and raped at a party during my sophomore year of high school. I was too scared to tell anyone about it, and I chose not to go to the police out of fear of what people would say about me. I blamed myself for getting so drunk, but I knew in my heart that my life was meant for more.

Shame grew in me as I forced myself to walk the halls of my high school, sharing the same space daily with my attacker. His actions were that of a hazing dare, one of two boys initiated into the "Cool Kids" group by forcing themselves on girls at parties. I was another statistic.

Something in me broke entirely, and I felt a yearning to seek out God like I never had before. I never told anyone what happened, but something sparked, and I knew I needed something different. I began going to a group, Young Life, a non-denominational youth group, where they taught about God in a nonthreateningly way. I started making friends with the other students on campus who went to Young Life, and my world began to open up. Despite my efforts to better my life and be different, I intensely struggled with suicidal thoughts and the desire to end it all.

Memories of the attack would flood my mind instead of restful thoughts producing sleep. The trauma was never addressed in my childhood and began to eat away at me. My feelings about everything intensified. Even though I participated in Young Life, it was a band-aid. I needed much more resounding help than singing a few songs and attending a youth camp. I tried so hard in my strength to manage my emotions. I lived a duplicitous life: Young Life on Tuesdays and hard-core partying, drinking, and inappropriate behavior the rest of the week. I was in so much pain without the words to talk about it.

A Doctor Without All the Information

I eventually went to a doctor and spoke with them about these intense feelings without discussing any potential causes. I was 17 years old when I was diagnosed with bipolar disorder. The doctor explained that I tended to have mood swings ranging from manic to depression. The doctor insisted that I could live a relatively "normal" life with medication.

Let me stop for a moment and say that I firmly believe that doctors are within God's plan and that their insights and discoveries can be God-inspired revelation. I think God loves doctors and science and thoroughly enjoys revealing mysteries to advance discovery. I did not know then that spiritual attack and warfare can manifest in physical ways that can be misinterpreted as something else. I took my diagnosis as fact instead of taking it to my creator. If I had, I would have discovered much earlier that I was never bipolar. Instead, I began my two-decade battle with creating a chemically balanced ecosystem in my body. This feat would prove to be huge since the chemicals could not treat the real problem.

Along with this diagnosis came the connotation that I was broken, less than, and would never quite measure up. Society frowned upon the term "bipolar" and instead viewed those suffering from that imbalance as crazy, lunatics, or unfit for responsibility and leadership. Those individuals trying to survive and thrive with a bipolar diagnosis had always been looked at as flawed, not quite right. I was ashamed of my presumed disability and was in a constant internal struggle for how to get through each day.

Broken But Loved

I began to feel trapped in my world and crave any way out. As my high school years closed, I prepared to venture into the real world to make something of myself. I opted to move to Los Angeles, California, where I could create enough distance from my childhood in Sacramento but keep close to my extended family living in Southern California. I was looking for a fresh start.

I started attending community college and juggled three jobs to help pay for everything. I worked in the restaurant industry as a hostess and server and as a teacher's assistant and camp counselor in the educational field. From the outside, it looked like I had it together. I would force my body to go through the motions daily, going to school, work, then back home to study.

The pressure of my schedule and the overwhelming nature of everything I was part of created increased anxiety and stress as I worried about paying bills and completing homework on time. I drank heavily to relieve my stress and numb the tensions, trying to escape the pressure. This excessive drinking led to lowered inhibitions, which made me regret many choices.

My self-esteem was tanked, and I had lost my identity. I found myself in relationships with men who treated me poorly and took advantage of me. My relationships riddled with lies, infidelity, and emotional abuse.

More Wrong Choices

I had finished my time at Santa Monica City College and transferred to California State University Northridge to get my bachelor's degree and Teaching Credential. I was 21 years old, dating a man eight years older. This man, Mr. LA, was part of the entertainment industry. After a short time of dating, I found out I was pregnant. As I struggled with the possibility of becoming a parent- responsible for another human- Mr. LA was researching luxury abortion clinics. We called our parents, and all parties suggested aborting. I felt like I had no options. I felt like I was all alone. I cried for days at a time, feeling so trapped and alone. Mr. LA scheduled and took me to the appointment.

I told him I did not want to do it if I was at least six weeks pregnant. As I lay on the table, I cried. I knew in every moment that I was making the wrong choice, but no part of me could stand up and say stop. The nurses gave me medicine to sleep, and as I went under, I heard one say, "Oh look, she's barely pregnant. Only six weeks".

I woke up after the procedure empty, with a soul shape scrapped out. They had taken any hope of everyday life with happiness and success along with my baby. I was devastated. I remembered the last comment from the nurses. The outpatient procedure left deeper, more permanent scars than I could have imagined, etching my mistakes inside my bones seemingly displayed for all to see.

I tried to pick myself back up and move on, but my guilt and regret were overwhelming. I began to sabotage myself as I felt I did not deserve to live. The enemy took my choices and used them to create a playlist of negative comments meant to strap me into a lifestyle of depression, mania, and suicidal thoughts. He used my circumstance and my thoughts against me. I felt lost, alone, and incapable of redemption.

God did not want me to continue to live under the pressure of the guilt and regret that had consumed me. It would be 15 years before I discovered that God was not too disgusted with me. He does not run from my horror. The abortion almost broke me, but I believe God uses it for His glory.

When I opened myself up to reclaim my identity through the eyes of God, the Holy Spirit dropped a verse in my Spirit.

Bless the Lord, O my soul;

And all that is within me bless His holy name!

Bless the Lord, O my soul, and forget not all his benefits:

Who forgives all your iniquities, Who heals all your diseases,

Who redeems your life from destruction,

Who crowns you with loving-kindness and tender mercies,

Who satisfies your mouth with good things,

So that your youth is renewed like the eagles.

Psalm 103: 1-5

I am forgiven, and my past choices do not have to define me. My life is redeemed, and I'm renewed.

Working All Things Together

Prominent memories dig deep in our being and imprint a snapshot of circumstance and emotion. Each time a significant event, good or bad, gets imprinted and etched, it can change the direction or trajectory of our lives. Many years later in a Trauma Informed Classroom professional development, I would learn what trauma does to the body; how trauma can rewire and reconfigure our brains and physical makeup. That discovery was vital on the journey the Holy Spirit had me on.

After the abortion, I spent another year and a half in Los Angeles. I struggled with identity and knowing my true self. The relationship with Mr. LA was on and off for the entire time. I felt trapped and alone. I wanted my relationship to work out, but I felt like something was wrong. The enemy continued to torment me with my self-generated playlist of insults, accusations, and labels. Through those 18 months, I spent a handful of nights on the suicide hotline with friendly individuals who talked me through the night. Nights were always the worst torment. Living alone did not help. Each time I felt more drained and more alone.

In one of the "off" times with Mr. LA, I was desperate not to be alone at night and move in with a man I barely knew in a brand-new dysfunctional relationship. When we moved in together, he threw a hot baking tin fresh out of the oven at me from across the room. In that moment, I received clear understanding of an immediate need for change.

Go Home

I began to feel a sense of urgency to get out of the situation. Searching for something that would ground me and help me feel myself again, I finally decided to move back to Sacramento and start back from what I knew. At the time, I still did not have a close relationship with the Holy Spirit. I did not know how to decipher His voice; I did not realize that the Holy Spirit was using all of my mess for good. He was guiding me out of the muck. As I have gone on this journey of healing with the Holy Spirit, I am confident now that He was with me, nudging and guiding me without me realizing it.

It was a month or so from when I decided to move back to when the semester finished and I could relocate. I spent that month couch hopping from friend to friend because I had no place to live. Finally, I moved back in with my mom in Sacramento and crashed on my little brother's floor.

In the meantime, Mr. LA and I had rekindled our relationship and had decided to attempt a long-distance relationship, just a quick flight from Los Angeles to Sacramento. I thought this would help us work on our issues, but the writing was on the wall.

No Smooth Transitions

A month passed, filled with job applications, interviews, and rejections. I was too qualified for the restaurants I was applying for, and none of the super fancy places were hiring. It was the end of January 2008, and the pressure to find a job was overwhelming. I walked back into PF Changs China Bistro in Downtown Sacramento to follow up on the application I had dropped off the week before. I asked to speak to the manager. He started on the familiar spiel- I was overqualified, so I would not be fulfilled- he believed I would get bored quickly. I cut him off and begged for the opportunity. I did not want to spill my sob story of a fresh start, but I gave just enough clues to convince him that despite being overqualified, I would love the opportunity.

Something in me knew I had to plead my case that day. I believe the Holy Spirit helped me with that. At the time, I had no idea that this would be such a monumental chapter in my life that was compact and lasted less than six months.

God Brings Me a Gift

I was offered the job, with some reluctance on the hiring manager's part. I started training immediately. As part of training, new servers must do some shifts in the expediting window. In the kitchen area where the chefs plate the food, the front-of-house staff puts plates on trays to deliver to the tables—the key to getting familiar with the food at the restaurant. As the expediter, I was traying food for all the other servers.

I was starting to get into a groove when two college guys walked up to me. Decked out in PF Changs serving attire, they approached me.

"Oh wow! You sure are beautiful!" said the tall one.

Oh no, here we go. I realized they were hitting on me, for which I had no time. My life was already complicated, and I had a boyfriend. I politely shot them down and continued with my shift.

The tall one circled back. "You will need to make some friends here eventually. Just come out with a group of us to get to know everyone. We are all going after work. Just stay for one drink," he said. He made seemingly valid points.

When the shift ended a few hours later, I walked to the Bistro around the corner. Upon arrival, I saw the tall guy, Austin, and one of the female bartenders. I went in and sat down at their designated part of the bar. Austin ordered me a drink, and we all started talking. The female bartender consumed her drink and left within 10 minutes of me arriving. I later found out that Austin had bribed the female bartender to come to have a drink. He was bound and determined that he was going to get to know me. This persistence would serve him well and would become a foundation for us.

I found almost immediately that I had a connection to Austin. I had not given him the time of day while we were working, but as I sat there talking with him, I felt as if my soul had found fresh air. We had so many things in common, despite drastically different childhoods. He was a pastor's kid raised in the church, and I came from brokenness.

Our connections continued to mount as the hours passed. The last call at the bar prompted us to relocate to the car for more conversation. It was as if my soul was being fed for the first time in my whole life. The sun rose that next morning as we talked in the car. Realizing we both had shifts in a few hours, we said our goodbyes, departed ways, and went home.

I had no idea what he was honestly thinking, but I knew I felt a stirring in my Spirit about Austin. I drove to my mom's house and called Mr. LA.

"I fell in love with someone last night. I am not sure how he feels, but I know I have to end this relationship to give that one a fair shot," I said.

At the time, I did not realize that Austin, the Vice President of his fraternity, was meeting with one of his fraternity brothers for breakfast, where he confessed to his brother that he believed I was the woman he would marry. The man whose mantra was "girlfriends are diseases" was actively professing to his closest friend that he wanted to marry me. This shocking statement was a complete game-changer shift in the trajectory of Austin's life.

New Beginnings

"I'm single," I said as I optimistically greeted Austin just 8 hours after our last encounter.

"No, you're not," he claimed with a sense of understanding that we had chosen each other. "Wanna hang out after our shift later?"

This was the beginning of what would turn out to be a whirlwind love story that is always a showstopper. The cliff notes version is that we never separated after that. I went to his house after work that day, and we have been together ever since. Our connection rapidly increased, and I felt complete when I was with him. On January 25, 2008, I met Austin on my third day of work. We found an apartment together three weeks later and rescued a puppy. Within two months, we got engaged.

In May of 2008, we went to dinner with Austin's parents. We told them about our idea to have a wedding the following summer. As pastors, they were not super excited about us "living in sin" as it was obvious that the young 21- and 23-year-olds were engaging in premarital activities.

I have to pause the story here for a moment, as one of the spots where I can see now how the Holy Spirit was working things together. I am thankful for the relationship that Austin's parents have with God and the Holy Spirit. Austin's parents recognized me as God's match for their son despite being a broken mess. With their encouragement, we moved the wedding date to the following weekend.

What was the rush? No rush; instead, perfect timing. We asked if Austin's dad would marry us in our apartment the following weekend.

I made a cape for our dog, and she acted as our ring bearer. On June 8, 2008- less than five months from when we met, with just our parents and siblings as witnesses, we were married in our apartment with a poster of Biggie Smalls in the background.

We immediately began settling into married life. Austin, who at 21 was the youngest employee in company history to move up so quickly, had advanced himself from a busser to entering the management program. He took part-time classes at Sacramento State University to get his Bachelor of Arts in communications and progressed through the management program quickly and easily.

Meanwhile, Austin suggested that I quit my job at the restaurant and focus on my schooling. I had transferred to Sacramento State to finish my teaching credential and was in the student teaching portion of my degree. My schedule required me to teach during the days and take classes at night. Austin insisted that we prioritize my education so that I could get my foundation for my career.

My marriage to Austin is the most significant proof of the Holy Spirit being involved in my life even before I knew who the Holy Spirit was. Many people assumed I was pregnant or just young and dumb when I chose to marry a man I hadn't known long. I even had some family claim he was using me and would leave me quickly after he got bored. Has our marriage been perfect? No, but is our marriage God-inspired? Absolutely so.

We have come a long way in our marriage, and part of that journey has been a reconfiguration and putting God at the center. Trusting that God brought us together to become a power couple for the kingdom has helped us rediscover who we are in Christ. This has dramatically impacted my growth in discovering my identity as a daughter of the One True King and finding my purpose in advancing the kingdom.

Tsunami Effect

As a young married woman, I now had a partner to walk through life. I had discovered that God knew what He was doing when he matched me with a man from a family of pastors. When I married into the Preston family, I married into a biblically led family that understood the power of prayer, fellowship with the Holy Spirit, and the grace and empowerment that goes along with a life with Jesus. It would be these people who helped shape me in my next season and help me grow into who I was to be.

In my early 20s, I was diagnosed with bipolar and depression. I was encouraged to take medication to help with the problems of the diagnosis. I wanted to try to handle it on my own, so I chose not to take medicine and instead found myself self-medicating. As I progressed through school and the challenges of adulthood, I found myself trying to numb my senses and find ways to escape. Alcohol became a frequent consumption.

Masking Hurts

On our first Thanksgiving as a married couple, we spent the day with each of our sets of parents. First, we spent time with Austin's parents in Rio Vista and then drove the 60+ minutes to visit my dad in his new home in Loomis. I dreaded the part at my dad's, as I was not a massive fan of his new wife. This new wife was the woman with whom he created his second family, while he was supposed to be part of his original family. I was going to spend Thanksgiving with my homewrecker. I woke up requesting a mimosa. I could feel the pressure mounting the entire day.

I look back on that day and feel sorry about my decisions, and I wish I had stayed in bed. The enemy tried to take me out that day, and I almost let him. Uncomfortable family dynamics and inappropriate conversations led to mind-numbing amounts of vodka and wine, sending me into a complete breakdown. After hours of drinking in every location of my day, Austin insisted we head home.

As he helped me to bed, I began screaming and yelling, sobbing violently and uncontrollably. I cried about being possessed by demons and wanting to die. Not knowing what to do, he called his parents for prayer. As pastors, his parents, well versed in the topic of spiritual warfare, saw it for what it was, not just a drunken night but a full-blown enemy attack. They drove an hour in the middle of the night to come to lay hands on a drunk girl, their new daughter-in-love. It was dramatic and messy, and I was ashamed for many reasons. I allowed the enemy to use that to torment me and make me feel like I did not deserve someone like Austin.

This is another moment where the Holy Spirit revisited with me. He has helped me understand what was happening that day and why it was so impactful. He has helped me see that the enemy was using the past hurts to create a tsunami in my life. The Holy Spirit showed me that I was relying on alcohol to push past instead of relying on Him to work through my pain and suffering. This woman was the woman that showed up at my doorstep six months pregnant with news that our family was breaking apart for good when I was the age of 12. She found her way into my life and my family, without my permission, to the detriment of my stability. I had wrapped up the pain of my childhood in the existence of this person. I had allowed myself to be consumed with emotions and lose control. God heard the prayers of my new parents, and the Holy Spirit worked on my behalf. I genuinely believe that something shifted for me that night. I knew there was more to God, and I was beginning to see that I had married into something different from where I came.

I felt emotionally drained with no fundamental understanding of how to heal. I was so close to the answer but had no idea how to tap the empowerment of the Holy Spirit. Something about my new parents and their ability to see the good in me caught my attention. I was unsure what it meant, but I knew I was on some journey. I could not have expected or predicted the precise details of this journey that I have been on, but I believe that was one of the first realizations that there was more, and my new parents knew something about it.

What's In Your Body?

The complete meltdown prompted me to contact a doctor, who officially talked me into beginning medications to treat me for my diagnosed bipolar disorder. I was ashamed of how I had behaved and was determined to be "fixed." I was branded with the label, seared with the hot iron mark for all to see. Or at least that is what I felt. I felt exposed, broken, and absolutely out of control. It would be the beginning of a decade-long fight with pharmaceuticals. I had been prescribed three different medicines. One for depression, for mania, and one for sleep. Each medication brought with it a whole bunch of side effects and possible complications.

Meanwhile, I finished my teaching credential and graduated in December of 2008. I got hired to take over the first-grade position at a local elementary school starting the first of the year when we returned from winter vacation. It was a high-pressure situation for someone fresh out of school. I was walking into a situation where the retiring teacher would just bypass material when it got hard, and the students struggled. The results of that teacher's actions meant 17 "below basic" students out of 21 total students. I was in for a challenging experience.

I was getting into a routine and feeling some success. I felt like I was meeting the needs of my students, and I was mentally stimulated, but I was unhappy with the grade level. I was passionate about 6th grade and wanted to be a sixth-grade teacher, gathering inspiration for teaching from the teacher who changed my life, Mrs. L. Also, I was not a fan of the boogers on my legs, reminders of the loving embrace of all the school children each day.

God was at work, and within a few short weeks, a friend of Austin's reached out with a lead on a 6th-grade position in central California. We drove three hours to the town of Hanford, California, to interview for my second teaching position. They asked me to wait around to talk to the human resources director and offered me a job on the spot after a few short hours! We drove home the three hours, elated at this new adventure but with no proper understanding of the adventure we were about to embark on.

New Developments

As we anxiously wrapped up the school year and began planning to move our lives 300 miles away, we got some unexpected news. It was the middle of May, and the year was closing. All the regular activities that signal the end of a school year were commencing. It was understandable to be tired, but my teaching partners insisted I seemed overly tired. On May 18, just three weeks shy of our first wedding anniversary, I purchased three different brands of pregnancy tests and kindly requested to use the Target bathroom. In the Target bathroom, I discovered I was pregnant with our first child.

I was elated and terrified! We had talked about a family, but here it was right in front of me. The celebratory baby was conceived the night we got back from my job interview. I rushed back to the store and purchased an "I love Daddy" onesie, excited to share the news with Austin. I took my new purchase back home, got dressed, packaged it up, and drove to the restaurant where Austin was managing. I waited for a few moments before he found me and settled me in at the bar.

I anxiously gave him a hand-wrapped shoebox covered with tissue paper. As he opened the lid and exposed the contents, the expression on his face changed, and tears began to stream from his eyes as the reality of this new life hit him. He was just as excited as I was. Our combined elation seemed to bring us deeper together, and I thought for the first time that I had finally made it. I had a career, and I was starting my family. I was sure that this was the beginning of something great.

This Isn't Happening

Unbeknown to me, my developing baby was in severe danger. My lifestyle and medications were not creating a happy and healthy environment for a fetus to grow and develop appropriately. That next week I had a doctor's appointment with my psychiatrist, with whom we shared the news. "You will need to abort immediately," he said. The doctor spent the next forty-five minutes discussing all the congenital disabilities this unborn baby could have due to my medications for bipolar disorder.

"No spine"…" may live to birth, but not much longer"… I could hear the comments, but my mind was spinning. My whole life, I wanted to grow up, get married, and have a family. I had gone in the right "order," getting married and having the baby. But here I was with this devastating news. My immediate thought was that I had done this to myself. I had caused this curse on my life by aborting the first baby that I was ever pregnant with. I had brought this cycle onto my family that would prevent me from living the ultimate dream and creating the type of life for myself that I never had as a child, safety and security in a family unit with a mom and dad and kids.

The doctor was adamant that this would be a failed pregnancy. We were at a loss and completely wrecked. We could barely think straight, but Austin suggested we pray. Although my grandmother was Catholic, and I went to a catholic school for four years, I never really did feel comfortable praying. We were taught to pray to Mary on many occasions, which did not sit right with me. As Austin led us in prayer, we sobbed and begged for the healing power of the Holy Spirit. I had never heard my husband pray in such a way.

God Confirms

I went to take a shower. I put on some music and got in. As I sat with the hot water running over my head, I cried to God, "Please, Lord, I don't know what to do, but if you fix this, I will do anything."

An overwhelming sense of calm overcame me, and I felt a warm wrapping sensation, as if I were getting a full hug. No audible voice spoke, just an understanding deep within myself, a simple knowing, "You will carry that baby to term, and he will be a strong man of God" the Holy Spirit spoke to my Spirit. At that moment, a song came on the radio which would act as an anthem of hope for our young family.

Be strong in the Lord and,
Never give up hope,
You're going to do great things,
I already know,
God's got His hand on you, so,
Don't live life in fear,
Forgive and forget,
But don't forget why you're here,
Take your time and pray,
These are the words I would say.

These Are the Words I Would Say- Sidewalk Prophets

I did not know how to explain it, but I knew we would be ok. It would be two more weeks before we could see our baby on the ultrasound machine to confirm viability.

It was one of the most challenging parts of my life up until this point. It took me many years to indeed be able to talk about it. In hindsight, it is interesting that the enemy was able to use what the world said about me to create a perceived need for medication, resulting in an attempt to take out me and my offspring. I did not realize it at the time, but I allowed the enemy to latch on and place blame for the scare on my need for medication. In my journey through understanding, the Holy Spirit has brought me back to this time in my life to process that it was not just about me. The Holy Spirit had helped me to see that He has his hand on the lives of my offspring from even before they arrived.

Visalia

We packed up our apartment and two dogs and migrated to our new home in early June 2009. After moving into a cute three-bedroom house with no air conditioner and a gas leak, we quickly found a better option in a three-bedroom apartment with an air conditioner and a pool. I was in heaven! As the summer continued, I began attending training and professional developments in anticipation of the new school year with the new grade level and an increased number of students.

I was nervous and feeling out of my element. The enemy began working in my head, telling me I was not good enough and would fail. I had yet to tell my new employer that I was pregnant and would be needing maternity leave within my first six months on the job. I was terrified that that would be grounds for termination. The thought even crossed my mind that I would have to choose between a career and motherhood. I began to panic.

God Brings Me Another Blessing

My phone rang. It was my new teaching partner. I have to stop the story here and say that God places certain people in your life for a reason. Lori was God-inspired. Everything about her was what I needed. She became my work wife and my best friend. Just a few years older than me with two small children of her own, she was in the phase of life I was walking into. She was a pastor's wife at a local church.

Full of fear, I told her I was pregnant. She screamed with excitement and began talking about what a blessing it was. I got the same sense of the Holy Spirit acting at that moment, and I felt a connection to her. From that moment on, she always had my back. It would be years later until I could finally say what she was to me. Lori was my first spiritual model. She was so pretty, put together, and was as sweet as could be. She was also unapologetically Christian. She had a Christian background and raised her family in a Christian home. I watched as she navigated challenging problems in her life and how she relied on God and the Holy Spirit to get her through. The truth is, she was the "coolest godly woman" I knew. Until that point, I had limited examples of what a godly woman was; it was inspirational.

Later in life, Lisa Bevere would explain these spiritual models as necessary in a new believer's walk. She was right. It took me over a decade to realize how monumental Lori was in the story of who I am and how I came to reclaim my identity. It was through finding strength in watching choices that Lori made that helped me see that mainstream was not the only way.

Lori and Adam introduced us to the church we attended while living in Visalia, California. When Axel was finally born, and it was time to dedicate him, we knew that Lori needed to be part of his story. Lori became a Godmother to Axel, but in all actuality, she was also a spiritual Godmother to me too.

Our time in Visalia was short-lived, just a blip on the radar of life. The most impactful things may not take much time to progress through. After Axel was born, we only spent another 15 months in Visalia before relocating back to Northern CA to be with family. We were in Visalia for less than two years, but the memories and lessons from that time in our lives are very impactful and are huge milestones in our journey.

Another One on the Way

While in Visalia, I remained off medicine for bipolar. In December of 2010, I found out I was pregnant with our second child. We were shocked! Axel was only eleven months old when we discovered God had blessed us with another. I thought back to the early days of marriage when my twenty-three-year-old self wanted four children, all before the age of thirty, and realized this is what I had asked for. Here I was about to get what I wanted, what I had prayed for, what I felt my purpose was.

As the weeks went on, my emotions went out of whack. Life events happened, and the symptoms of bipolar and depression began to rear their ugly head—attacks from all sides. My emotions took control, and I became a shell of a person. I was unable to function without crying daily. Doctors blamed the pregnancy and the bipolar diagnosis.

Things were heating up at work with new mandates and state standards changing. I had a challenging class, and I was feeling defeated. Austin was finishing up school with a completion date of March 2011. He got a job to begin in February 2011, in which he would be traveling along a territory in California to interact with the company's customers. This commuting sometimes kept him traveling for days at a time without coming home. Things seemed to be falling into place for Austin but out of place for me. He was doing everything he could to provide for our young family, but it meant that we saw each other even less, and I became even more of a single mom.

Our lease was up, and with Austin's constant commuting, my growing belly, my increased out-of-control emotions, and the baby I already had, I was beginning to need some help. Thankfully, I did have some cousins that lived in the area with an In-Laws' Suite in their home. In February 2011, Axel and I moved into their home to finish the school year with the intention to move back to Northern California in June of that year.

As I leaned on my cousins' support and Lori's support, I attempted to navigate the waters of being a pregnant single mom. Until then, Axel had never been to day care or in the care of anyone besides Austin or me. Austin was his primary caregiver during the day and then had been working nights. I would be Axel's primary caregiver at night and work during the day.

Emergency Changes

Axel was enrolled in daycare just a quick drive from my school. I was fragile, walking around like a heavy gust of wind might shatter me. Each day I felt more depleted and out of control until I got a phone call. I needed to pick up Axel immediately; it was an emergency.

Emergency protocols were in place; I left my class and rushed to my baby. When I arrived, the police notified me that the daycare was shut down immediately for the shaken baby syndrome. A young girl who attended the daycare was in the hospital with signs of shaken baby syndrome, which was traced back to our daycare. I was devastated. I immediately felt the anxiety grip me. My heart stopped, and I could not breathe. The officer informed me of signs to look for in my child. As the reality settled that my son was not safe, I began to lose it. My emotions took over, and I began to sob. In hindsight, the officer probably assumed the extra feelings were due to my pregnancy as he tried to console me and encourage me to go home and rest with my baby.

I grabbed my baby and drove home. Despite knowing my son was now safe with me, I had no idea if any damage was done to my baby or his brain. I could not make sense of the information I had been given that day. My mind was swimming with emotions, and I could feel myself losing control. I called Lori and could not speak, only sob. Knowing something was wrong, she drove to my cousin's house to check on me. When she arrived, she found me crying uncontrollably in a ball on my bed. She helped me call my doctor and took care of

Axel while I discussed the immense sadness and anxiety I was feeling with my doctors.

After an hour on the phone with my doctors and no reprieve from crying, they suggested that I begin taking Zoloft, a medicine intended to help with depression and extreme sadness. Still traumatized by being told to abort my first baby due to taking medications while pregnant, I was adamantly against taking any medications while pregnant. My doctors kept insisting, but I was firmly against it. Lori prayed with me and asked the Holy Spirit to work on my behalf. I knew I was not in control, but something in me told me not to take medicine. I believe the Holy Spirit took that moment and guided me. Looking back, the feeling of letting go of control of that situation because it was too much to deal with as a human was one of the Holy Spirit-inspired moments where He was leading. I finally settled down and was able to stop crying.

Stuck Between a Rock and a Hard Place

Due to the daycare shut down, I needed another option to help take care of Axel during the day while I was teaching. We had no options and were very limited on finances, so when my mother-in-law offered to help, we knew this was our best option. Austin came the next day to pick up my fifteen-month-old baby and take him to his mother's house, three hours away from me. I knew this would be hard, but I did not know what other option I had. I needed to get through the school year, and then we would be ok. Just keep moving forward.

That seems so much easier to say than done. The next day, when Austin arrived to get Axel, the tears started to flow. At first, a trickle that I could not get to stop quickly turned into a hyperventilating sob. We packed up Axel's things, and I kissed him goodbye. Austin drove away, and I collapsed. I felt like my whole world had been ripped away from me instantly. Every comfort was gone. I was alone and so very depressed. The tears never stopped.

Days passed, and I was a shell of a person. I was unable to eat, sleep or work. I spent hours on the phone with the doctors. Eventually, it was decided that I was unfit to function in my usual capacity. I was placed on immediate medical disability and released from my contract position. The need to be removed cut me deep. I felt less of a human being. I felt like I was not good enough to handle life. Something in me snapped, creating a traumatic scar deep inside my being.

Trauma Scars are Stopping Points

This trauma would be a stopping point on my journey with the Holy Spirit. It was a touch point in my life where the Holy Spirit was with me and helping guide me, but I did not know and did not hear His voice. He was opening and closing doors, but I was not walking with God, so I was not hearing His guidance.

In March 2011, at 22 weeks pregnant I moved back to Rio Vista, California, to be with Austin and Axel. I was broken and needed the support of my family.

Medicine

Upon arrival, I was immediately put on bedrest and told to stay off my feet. The doctors were worried about my mental state, and so was I. As my due date neared, my moods fluctuated dramatically. My doctors urged me to consider medicine as soon as I delivered. Because I did not want the drug in my breast milk, I would be unable to nurse my baby. The enemy used this to attack me and make me feel like I was not a full mother, unable to feed her baby the way God intended.

Once my son Ayzik was born, I committed to 6 weeks of nursing him before starting the medicine. The count down was on to me creating my cocktail of medications determined by my team of doctors for my intense bipolar episodes. On paper, I was a hot mess. It was the beginning of a nine-year roller coaster of mismanagement of my health.

Bipolar disorder is a spectrum disorder that contains mania and depression. Everyone diagnosed with bipolar has common "tells," but each human is different, and the disorder affects them differently. For my particular brand of bipolar disorder, I was diagnosed with severe depression and mania. My mood swings would fluctuate from intense happiness on rare occasions to deep despair where every part of my body ached with longing and crippling sadness. I was prone to anxiety attacks that would increase over the nine years, eventually resulting in acquiring a service dog.

When experiencing a manic episode, I would be known to lose track of time, pace uncontrollably, and even go on spending sprees. One such time resulted in me spending over one hundred and fifty dollars at the Dollar Store. This was not within our budget at the time and was one of Austin's first big red flags that increased his involvement in me seeking the correct help for what was ailing me. Austin spent the next several years studying me. As I tried different options, Austin documented the effects on my moods, how I was functioning as a person, and my ability to understand what was happening to me.

I believe that God works through doctors. I think medicine is not inherently wrong, and there are many reasons to take the appropriate medication. That belief blinded me to the awareness that my prescription was not helping me. They were masking the symptoms of bipolar disorder. I never brought the diagnosis to God and asked for His clarification. I never knew that was something to do. Not until my journey began.

As I navigated through different medication regimens, I learned what masked the bipolar symptoms best. I found myself on the highest doses of all my medicines. As the years passed, I eventually maxed out on dosages and was taking twenty-two pills in one day. Getting my pills ready for the week was a weekly chore that required three different weekly pill containers and six daily alarms. Despite the high doses of chemically created medicines that were meant to help me, I found that I continued to need more. There was always something missing.

Eww, what's wrong with you?

I was told by a doctor that I was bipolar. In my limited understanding, the diagnosis seemed to fit. I was labeled with a letter far worse than a scarlet letter. This label told the outside world I was crazy, unstable, and on the brink of a padded cell. In our world, there remains a considerable stigma associated with bipolar disorder. Chemical imbalance is generally looked down on and seen as a weakness. That which is out of the control of the individual is held against them.

My first mistake was not taking that diagnosis to my Heavenly Father. Instead, I tried to find a way to live with it. What does living with it look like? It meant making sure to take my medicine every day and on time, hide when I felt like my medication was not working, and slowly try and change the stigma that bipolar had gained. I worked hard to educate those around me about the ability to live as a productive member of society while living with a chemical imbalance. I was doing everything I could to learn about this imbalance and how it affected my body.

Increasing Anxiety

I found myself as the unofficial spokesperson for the bipolar community. I empathized and became an advocate for others. I felt the legitimacy of the world seeing validity and importance in the bipolar community rested on my shoulders and would be based on how I interacted with others. This was a massive amount of pressure to contain. As I opened up about my bipolar, my anxiety began to increase until, one day, I had a massive panic attack at school that prevented me from doing my job successfully.

This panic attack left me pacing, stumbling, and unable to get a complete thought out, let alone teach new concepts. It may not have been evident to the students, but my body felt out of control. I thought I was going to explode. These panic attacks increased in frequency, location, and duration. Within a year of my first big panic attack in class, it was determined by a doctor that a service dog could be a supportive tool for me. It was something I had considered in the past but not something I thought I would ever experience. I had seen many people with service dogs and had gotten their views on how helpful they were. I was torn at the thought that I qualified. The enemy used that to attack my character and ability to make a difference for the kingdom. Having such a unique medical tool meant I must have severe enough anxiety to warrant another living thing following and tasking every move. I felt a weird sense of peace that I would be getting some help but felt exposed and more diminutive because it was a tool I needed.

Making a Way

As I did more research, God began to open all the doors. I started learning about dogs that do best with psychiatric service work and what types of characteristics are best. At school, one of my teaching partners also dabbled in helping families interact with dog breeders to purchase specific breeds of dogs. One of the breeds she worked with was a breed recommended for psychiatric work because of the immense bond they create with their owners- a Bichon Frise.

Armed with our new knowledge, a connection to a breeder, and a doctor's recommendation, our family began purchasing a dog to be trained as a service dog. God provided the resources for us to afford the cost of the dog and placed people in our lives that gave us information on how to proceed with the adventure. In January 2018, we brought home a fluffy little ball of hair and started the new season of growth and discovery. This 8-week-old ball of fluff would spend the next few months and years bonding with me, learning about me, helping me learn about myself, and being a physical representation of God's love for me. I know a huge part of my growth this last season is that I was willing to slow down and be obedient to God's leading- I am very thankful that God also chose to use an animal to help me understand.

God Uses Dogs

God used Kodah to not only help me through my anxiety attacks, but Kodah became a tool to help me refocus my attention and lean into God. I knew God had made way for this through the many steps it took to have everything ready. Things fell into place quickly and easily, resulting in a smooth process. Kodah started intense training right away, which entailed spending every possible moment with me, and was the equivalent of two-a-days like in Austin's high school football career. An early morning training before we left for school, an early afternoon training if we got home early enough, and/or an evening training in place of dinner. Although he did not go to school with me for the first six months, he was with me in some activity every other waking moment. At the time, I thought I was training a dog. As God has taken me on this journey, He has revealed that He was using that experience to refine me and sharpen my tools for the next season in life. Even as I write this book, God reveals to me how he orchestrated the different aspects to work together for good. I sit here in awe of the minute details that can be observed. Every attention to detail was paid in getting me to where I am now.

Relationships Grow

The responsibility of continued guiding, training, and being invested in another being has opened my eyes to the amount of love that God has for me. I continue to see a different side of my Heavenly Father. Even from the beginning, I could feel God was working on me, and I was inspired and motivated to learn more about Him. As I got closer to Kodah, I felt like my relationship with God was growing too because I understood His perspective more. I am finding that God used Kodah to help me discover more about myself and what made me who I am. I relied on Kodah as I learned about myself and revisited painful memories from my past.

Isaiah 58:11 states that Where God guides, He provides.

God guided me through this journey of revelation and provided a physical companion to help me process what I was learning about myself and how that would impact the next seasons of life and my legacy.

Training, Training, Training

Training continued, and at the start of the following school year, Kodah began going to school with me daily. He had a designated area in my classroom and began undergoing specialized training on campus before and after school to help with tasking while I was working. My anxiety had escalated, resulting in daily panic attacks while at work. One of the parents at the school was also an experienced dog trainer with an impressive resume that included training over one hundred service dogs privately and for the California Highway Patrol. We were introduced to him by the Assistant Principal, and we hit it off immediately.

He was a Christian, and our families shared similar values. He and his wife had a son in the same grade as our youngest. What started as a training relationship evolved into a true friendship. This friend continued to coach me and help me teach Kodah how to task for the entire time Kodah was training. He taught me how to bond and connect with Kodah in a way far deeper than I could have anticipated.

Kodah was learning how to recognize when I was becoming anxious and support me. Some of the most common tasks he would perform were body blocking in crowds, redirecting me with licking or jumping, and textile support. As my connection to Kodah deepened, and he began to anticipate my "episodes," he began providing relief to me more frequently. Although I was experiencing multiple anxiety attacks a day, Kodah was able to task and support me through them.

Hit the Fan

Kodah was settling into his new role with me when I got notified by my doctors that I would need to have foot surgery. As I recovered, this surgery would take me out of school for a few weeks. The first of two surgeries were scheduled for August 2019. Despite prearranging my long-term substitute for a three-week absence, I was pressured to come back after just two weeks due to behaviors in the class. This surgery which had my foot in a cast needing constant propping up, drastically slowed me down. I could not walk without assistive tools and was only allowed to walk for limited amounts before I would need to elevate my foot to help with swelling and pain.

Body proximity is when teachers redirect behaviors by simply being around the student. This might look like the teacher standing near a table that is heard talking for students to get back on task without a large scene being drawn. It is one of the teaching tools that you gain with time. This ability I had crafted well was not one at my disposal at this time.

In addition, the beginning of the year is when students look for their structure. Expectations are being set, and the year's success depends on the foundational understanding of how to behave and engage in class. I will admit that I took for granted what was engrained to be the natural building of successful expectations to help the students learn.

The substitute, although sweet as can be, lacked the years of experience that helped me craft this gift. I found myself confined to a desk with little support from the administration. The students noticed my weakness and took advantage of my vulnerability and inability to redirect and prevent misbehaviors from escalating. Students would ignore my directions and talk over me. I found it hard to manage the class and reached out to the administration for support.

To clarify the amount of time students were wasting in class talking, I once calculated over fifteen minutes of talking over me to socialize with friends. These kiddos were relentless. They saw an obvious opportunity to exploit the situation and took it. Instead of yelling at them in complete exasperation, I somehow waited patiently. It was over 15 minutes before anyone realized that they were being timed.

With no support from the administration and no clear plan for helping correct the behavior, I was on my own to provide a constructive consequence. Since the class spent the time socializing, I felt it reasonable to spend their allotted time for socializing, also known as fifteen minutes of recess, to make up the missed instructional minutes.

Enemy Attack

My choices to discipline my class and try to bring order back to the classroom so that I could do my job and educate the future were quickly matched with backstabbing plans to take me down on behalf of one of my room parents. I believe the enemy used this parent to launch the most significant attack on my mind, will, and emotions. This parent, with whom I had a few years of experience in multi-faceted ways, came after me with a vengeance.

This mom knew me as a teacher, as I had taught one of her older children, but she also knew me as a friend, as we had children the same age in the same class for a few years. We had a bond that I believe warranted vulnerabilities and openness. As someone who was in my inner circle to an extent, she knew of my struggles with bipolar and anxiety.

A devil-inspired group text message was created with all my classroom parents attached and sent out by this room parent. Detailed instructions of when and where to arrive at the district office to complain about me were sent out with scripted information about my alleged mental instability and inability to teach due to my bipolar and anxiety. This mom took all the personal information she knew about me and put it on blast for all my students' parents as a reason why the students lost recess at school. She felt so slighted and that her student had been mistreated that she set out to tear me down and rip apart everything I had ever worked for because of a fifteen-minute recess.

Out of Control

Events escalated, and my life at work felt like I was drowning. I was so confused and hurt. I thought this person was my friend, so I found myself fighting to prove my integrity and character and nursing the wounds of betrayal. In a particularly overwhelming moment, the weight of everything around me crushed me into a complete panic attack. The attacks were more frequent. The more verbal attacks and attacks on my character, the more panic attacks would grip me at the most inconvenient times. The enemy has a unique gift of building little things to become overwhelming, adding to the pressure cooker situation of my life at that moment. He would attack my mind and emotions without me even realizing he was there.

At that moment, I lost all control and had to release everything. There was no way I could be in control and in charge of something so big and messy. The allegations against me were unfair and a form of fighting dirty- it smelled of enemy attack from a mile away. I recognized it for what it was because the attack was so severe and yet so powerfully painful.

Pressing In

I began to press into God and ask for clarity and discernment. I knew I was way too small for something so big. The only one who could help me with any of it was God. Investigations continued, and work was so uncomfortably toxic. Although I was proved not to have been out of line with my punishments, the fact that my personal business was publicly used against me and with malice was exceptionally unsettling and made me feel exposed and uncomfortable. I was so incredibly broken and hurt.

The year progressed at a snail's pace, and finally, in March, the start of the third trimester, the whole world shut down for a global pandemic. Overnight, everything that we knew as usual changed. No more going to school. No more going to work. No more going to church. No more going to the grocery store.

Everyone went on lock down. Schools went virtual, and pajamas became the new school uniform. People found safety in their homes. I felt a stirring in me to press harder into God. My job got exponentially harder yet more manageable in some respects. Now, I had a mute button for every student. Many still lacked respect and desire to learn. New problems had arisen and proven to be a different kind of challenge. It was hard to keep them engaged, but it was easy to keep them quiet. The enemy tried to use a spirit of perfectionism to attack my beliefs of insufficiency about myself.

The World Shuts Down

Just like that, we were all forced to stay home. I found this part to be a blessing. I was no longer required to step foot on a campus where I felt exposed, taken advantage of, and disrespected. Just like that, I was given a reprieve from my tormentors. It proved to be a breath of fresh air of sorts. This global pause allowed me to distance myself from those who were hurting me the most. This pause allowed me to slow down enough and realize that God wanted more for me. God wanted me to be whole and healthy.

As the world tried to navigate the unknowns of the pandemic, I felt God was trying to talk to me. I could sense something stirring. Out of pure survival, I envisioned my home as a central calming space and asked God to help me feel safe and secure in my house. Our church offered services online, so we began watching Sunday services online. Thursday nights were Pursuit night, an hour-long service full of worship music and focused prayer. They started streaming these services online too.

After a few short weeks, I could feel the atmosphere in my home was noticeably different. I was feeling my relationship with God strengthen. My time in the secret place of prayer and communing with God was increasing, and I was learning more about the Holy Spirit and His part in the holy trinity. As we transformed our home, my hunger to know more about God, Jesus, and the Holy Spirit deepened. I found myself researching and studying the Holy Spirit and growing a relationship.

I realize now that this was the starting point of my healing and revival of my identity. I began pressing into biblically sound doctrine. I was hungry to learn more; I took as many bible study courses as possible through John and Lisa Bevere, Kris Valloton, and Havilah Cunnington. Two verses continued to run through all the studies I was learning.

> And do not conform to this world but be transformed by the renewing of the mind that you may prove what is good and acceptable.
>
> Romans 12:2
>
> Fix your mind on things above, not on earthly things.
>
> Colossians 3:2

These two verses continued to point me back to looking to Jesus, dwelling less on the circumstances of this world.

Truth In Doctrine

As I learned more about the Holy Spirit, I understood that He was there the whole time. As I learned about our calling as Christians to be kingdom-driven, eyes to the heavenly realm, I began to see that there was more to life and what God had in store for me. I knew I was in the change process, but I could not quite explain what was happening.

One such course was the Renew course through Messenger International. In this course, the Beveres led me through activities and scripture readings that helped me discover what God thinks about me. In addition, I began to see that I could do anything with God. I was getting stronger each day; each moment spent in the secret place was calling me closer to my breakthrough. I was growing my faith, exercising my faith muscles. I had discovered that God loved and wanted me: the good, the bad, and the ugly.

As I began to internalize the doctrine I was learning, I was inspired to continue my search to discover who God created me to be. I was finding that I had value hidden within the chaos of life. As I learned how to renew my mind and reclaim my identity, my relationship with the Holy Spirit strengthened, and I found a true friend. The Holy Spirit, the most ignored member of the Godhead, wanted to guide me. I had a breakthrough.

Breakthrough- The Journey Begins

"You are not bipolar," the Holy Spirit whispered to my spirit one morning. I had spent the last several days surrounding myself with praise and worship music, reading my bible, listening to podcasts, and reading books about renewing my mind. I was trying everything I could to prime myself and be ready for the Holy Spirit to guide my understanding. Something in me felt a procedural preparation that brought peace to learning the complex parts of my hurt. I truly believe the Holy Spirit prepared my heart for what I was about to discover.

"What do you mean," I questioned as my mind began to swim with the uncomfortable feeling of being deceived and dupped. My stomach dropped as my mind tried to process what was being said. In an instant, the sense of a heavy weight was being lifted from me. I knew in my heart that it was true, but I did not understand how I could have experienced all of what I had experienced.

"You never asked me if that was true. You were never called to take up that identity." The Holy Spirit assured my spirit.

Wait, what? My whole world was shaken and rocked to the core. My heart believed, but my mind began the task of double and triple-checking how that could be. I had never considered that the doctors were wrong or that I had been misdiagnosed. I was apprehensive about believing what I was hearing. I feared I was making it up; another enemy attack meant to drive me a little more crazy. I found myself on my face crying for clarification.

The Wrong Enemy

"You were never bipolar. You're not fighting the right enemy. Your battle is a spiritual one. You are using the wrong weapons," the Holy Spirit dropped a revelation of truth. I would spend the next year diving into understanding what this revelation meant.

As I tried to wrap my mind around a different identity, I was intrigued to get to the bottom of the deception. How was the enemy able to deceive me so well? Clearly, there was a problem, so if I was not bipolar, what is the actual problem? How do I attack what I cannot see? The more I discovered about the great deception, the more questions developed.

Masked Emotions

Rage. My emotions changed to rage. I do not know that there was any one thing I was feeling such intense anger toward, so the sentiment seemed out of place. Just moments ago, I had been feeling a sense of calm. This intrusive rage was a familiar feeling, and the Holy Spirit connected it to another experience in my life.

Less than a year prior, my brother had made some unfavorable choices in his life. Although those choices did not directly affect me, my reaction was this intense rage. When I learned the news, I felt it appropriate to have encountered this level of fierce emotion about a situation. As I sat with the Holy Spirit at that moment, He connected two dots- I had felt this level of emotion and rage many times before, and it was not healthy for me.

I was hooked! I wanted to know more about myself, and it seemed the only one who understood me was the Holy Spirit.

Crying Out

One day, in a blubbering mess of tears, I cried out loud, "Holy Spirit, show me my life. Take me on a healing journey to see how I acquired these feelings and beliefs about myself. Help me to heal from my wounds."

This honest and raw cry for help would launch me into an intense discovery of self. I knew I needed to identify the root of the problem before working through it. As I ventured the path of discovery, the Holy Spirit revealed that it was a problem with intense anger caused by generational strongholds and childhood traumas. I began my quest to learn about the stronghold of anger that had ravished my family and how it impacts lives. The perceived depression, manic episodes, and anxiety were all directly related to my inability to regulate and manage my intense emotions.

The problem was with control. I was letting my emotions control me. With a bipolar diagnosis, I could blame my intense emotions on a chemical imbalance. In reality, I needed training on how to manage my feelings. The irrational intensity of anger and pain regarding my brother's choices highlighted other areas of my life. Like playing whack-a-mole, the Holy Spirit brought up several instances where I had let my emotions boil over, a novice at containing them. I had let my feelings become toxic waste that I would spew at any person I perceived would be there to hurt me.

This resulted in poor communication with others, perceived running away from problems, and a general avoidance of the issues. My deficiencies have affected my relationships with others from the beginning of my life. I would get into situations where I was so mad that I felt like I would jump out of my skin. I would feel like a bull, seeing red, and would say or do things I would later feel ashamed of. I would be so emotionally overwhelmed that my body would cry to release the extra pressure, like an instant pot letting the steam out.

God Continues to be Faithful

I found myself digging into the word and any studies that would help me learn about the Holy Spirit and grow closer to God. As I learned more, I found my faith increasing. Those unfathomable miracles from the bible started to seem within the realm of possibility. I could feel my faith meter reading higher.

On one Sunday, our pastor was preaching about encountering God and the immediate changes that can occur through faith. He shared the story of the woman in Mark chapter five with a constant bleeding problem. She had been to many doctors and had gotten no improvements over the twelve-year ailment. Armed with just the knowledge of Jesus and the miraculous events, she insisted on working her way through the crowd to touch the bottom of his robe. She knew in her heart that simply touching Him could bring her healing. That is a lot of faith!

As the pastor wrapped up the story, "Daughter, your faith has made you well. Go in peace. Your suffering is over," the Holy Spirit gave me a vision of being the woman in the crowd. This verse was for me! My faith in God and His ability to renew and restore had healed me!

The pastor continued, this time telling the story in Mark 10:46 of blind Bartimaeus, who knew in his heart that Jesus could heal him instantly. In this story, blind Bartimaeus sits outside the city gates as Jesus walks by. When he hears that Jesus is coming, he immediately starts shouting requests for Jesus to have mercy on him. My Spirit jumped inside me as I felt connected to Bartimaeus, as I, too, had found myself blind to realities and crying out to Jesus for mercy in my life this season. Despite Jesus being all-knowing, He asks Bartimaeus what He can do for him. With all confidence, Bartimaeus announces that he wants to see. During service, God spoke to me again, saying, "You are Bartimaeus- your faith has healed you."

At that moment, I knew that faith was vital. I realized that I had given up all uneasiness and left it at the foot of Jesus. I had relinquished my healing and happiness and entirely relied on God. By doing so, I had opened myself up to receiving refreshing and restoration in my pressing into Him.

With God, You Can Do Anything

I can do all things through Christ who strengthens me.

Philippians 4:13

This verse has been one that has guided me over the last few years. I was taught it in one of my weak moments when I was looking for strength that I did not possess on my own. I had found my key to success; I needed to be strengthened by Christ. The natural next question was how I go about becoming strengthened by God.

Merriam Webster defines grace as unmerited divine assistance and virtue from God. While this is true, it is not the whole story. I have discovered that there are many facets to grace and what grace can do in our lives. Grace is the "Swiss Army Knife" of gifts God gives us.

John Bevere teaches about the grace of God. In his Holy Spirit-inspired teachings, he reveals that most Christians misunderstand the power of God's grace and often neglect the shackle-shattering empowerment of God's power. The neglect stems from a lack of discussion of what grace is. Many Christians know that God gives grace, but they are not sure what to do with that grace- how to harness it and use it for God's glory. Studying the biblically meaty topic of grace has given me a better understanding of obedience and walking in God's will.

Created for a Purpose

I have found that God created me for a purpose, and He is fully aware of my shortcomings. Through grace, He partners with me to accomplish what I could not achieve on my own. This includes slowing down, learning about myself, what He thinks about me, and using my God-given gifts to advance the kingdom. It includes God helping me quit drinking and breaking off generational strongholds of anger, addiction and anxiety from myself and my family. I am finding that God can use each part of my broken story to bring healing to others because of and through grace!

What I have experienced in my life may seem chaotic and traumatic. You would be right to assume it was hard and painful to experience. But now, I am uniquely qualified to help others through the muck and mire that life brings. The world is full of bad things, but I have become an overcomer. As I sit and ponder all the pain I have experienced, I find comfort in knowing that it will be used for good. It is through grace that I have this new understanding. It is through grace that I can be strong enough to continue discussing that which used to cripple me.

I must constantly remind myself of the biblical truth that I am not alone; God has my back and is working on my behalf. Instead of believing that I am doing things on my own, I have to make the conscious effort to fight my battles the way God has called me to, by putting on the armor of God and wielding the sword of truth. This requires me to dig into the Word of God and internalize biblical instruction for my life; including that through Christ, I am a new creation.

In reality, we will all have moments when the enemy tempts us. Even Jesus himself had to fight battles of temptation from the enemy. If Jesus did, so will I. I have to use the examples written about in scripture to see how Jesus handled himself and use that as a role model for my own life. Each time Jesus was tempted, He referred back to scripture. This has shown me that the Word of God is one of our most powerful tools.

I am a new creation!

Therefore, if anyone is in Christ, he is a new creation; old things have passed away.

2 Corinthians 5:17

Now, what?

So, you have realized that you are not alone. You sense a stirring in your spirit that you might have overlooked in the past. You have discovered that you may have been labeled with something that does not belong to you. You may even feel like your whole life has been a lie. What do you do now?

You find yourself ready to make a change and to learn what God says about you. Dear friend, I come alongside you to let you know that it is never too late to bring it to God. It takes surrender. A decision that you will stop trying to make things work on your own and submit to what God can do.

It all starts with a pressing into God. A decision you want to draw near to the presence of God to get that peace and understanding. As you press in, a few steps can help you on your journey.

Step 1: Get to know the Holy Spirit

The Holy Spirit is the most ignored member of the Godhead, yet is the one who comforts, brings healing, and guides. When I finally took the time to get to know Him, I truly felt connected to God. One of the most impactful studies that I ventured was the Holy Spirit: An Introduction course through Messenger International.

Each time I read that book I gain a deeper understanding of the many facets of the Holy Spirit and am more deeply in awe of how much He loves me. As I have learned more about the Holy Spirit, I find myself with a companion in every moment of every season of life. My world is so much more colorful and vibrant with Him by my side and at the center of my family and marriage.

I pray that you too feel the fruits of joy that only the Holy Spirit can provide.

STEP 2: Renewing your mind

A renewing of the mind is required to wash off the clouded judgment of how the world sees situations. Renewing the mind helps center your thoughts to be aligned with what God says about you and how God intends us to contribute to the building of the kingdom.

You see, you matter, and we need you. Each person has been given unique qualities meant to intertwine with the unique qualities of fellow believers to weave a tapestry of gifts to help shine God's light here on earth.

I started my process of renewing my mind by venturing through the Renew course through Messenger International. I took the time to do the journal prompts and say the declarations. After a few weeks, I could feel my mindset changing. As my perspective began to change, I was open to hearing what was happening.

Renewing the mind is a continuous step. Although I have grown and learned about myself, I still have to guard my mind against enemy attacks and continue to renew and refresh my thinking by staying in the word and seeking God's presence.

I pray that you too discover exactly what God says about you and what purpose He created you for. Get rid of the labels that others have put on you and find your true identity.

STEP 3: Bring it to God

Whatever has been said about you- medical diagnosis, evaluations, and judgments- take them up with God, your actual creator. Ask God if He agrees with the diagnosis, evaluation, or assessment. Sometimes the diagnosis is accurate, and you need to go to battle differently. By bringing things to God, we can formulate a successful battle strategy.

If you find what is being said about you is true, it may be a conviction that God is trying to help you grow through. This growth opportunity is getting you ready for something in your future. Acknowledging that conviction is the first step to trusting God to help you move past your current situation.

If you find what is being said about you false, God can remove the layers of deceit to reveal what is truly underneath. In my case, a misdiagnosis of bipolar was masking an unhealthy amount of anger resulting in anxiety and depression. Our bodies are so complicated. All of my symptoms were in line with a bipolar diagnosis, so it took me to go to my actual creator to find out what was wrong.

I pray that you too remember to bring everything to God. Every part of your life is important to Him. Open your heart and mind to His leading and providing of a battle strategy that is specific to your need.

STEP 4: Be Obedient

As you hear God guiding you, follow directions. Even if it seems silly, I have found that God is the most creative! He uses all kinds of situations for His glory. The more obedient I become in the small things, the more truth and revelation I gain to help me through life's trials and tribulations. As I surrender to behaving the way God has called me to act, He reveals my true identity and the unique gifts He empowered me with so that I could grow the kingdom.

As I felt led to do small things like pray for a particular person or event, I practiced obediently responding quickly. I found that I was learning His voice and what it felt like to be led by the Holy Spirit. Then I began to see that the desires of my heart were changing and I was feeling led to volunteer at church as part of the dream team. This slight stirring turned into our family helping launch a church plant.

As we got a few months under our belt, I began to feel a more intense calling to offer my time to help and teach kids. My husband and I brought this to our pastors, who revealed that they had been praying about us helping with the youth ministries. We accepted the offer and said YES to God to be the Youth Leaders for the church.

I pray that as you feel led by the Spirit you too have the courage to act obediently. Though this may feel uncomfortable at first, the more you act obediently the first time, the easier this becomes.

The Result

As the Holy Spirit has guided me through my healing journey, He has taken me by the hand to show me where he was with me the whole time, without me being completely aware. The immense closeness and longing I felt when I realized that God had been invested in me from the beginning were overpowering and intense. My journey is riddled with self-medication and seeking in the wrong locations, but I have overcome my circumstances and am walking into God's calling on my life.

Challenge:

Reclaim your own identity. It is time to begin your journey! Write out the significant events in your life and the immediate results. Look for God in a mess. Can you find where he was working behind the scenes?

Made in the USA
Las Vegas, NV
16 September 2024

95332357R10049